Vending

America's Best Kept Secret

by

Cool Water

Copyright © 2010 2020 Cool Water

All Rights Reserved

No portion of this book may be reproduced in any form, electronic or mechanical means, including information storage and retrieval systems, without written permission from the publisher. The only exception is a reviewer, who may quote short excerpts in a published review.

Published by: Artificially Flavored Entertainment: Atlanta, Georgia

Created in the USA
Cover Design: Avery McBride and Sarah Smith

TABLE OF CONTENTS

Introduction 1

Chapter 1— Getting Started..................................2

Chapter 2— When Things Go Bad 8

Chapter 3— Business Affairs................................11

Chapter 4— Accounting..12

Chapter 5— How Do I Locate Places for My Machine..14

Chapter 6— Lets Talk Percentages 17

Chapter 7— Non-Profit Organization...................19

Chapter 8— You and The Owner Don't Agree 22

Chapter 9— Strategic Planning.............................24

Chapter 10— Conclusion.......................................26

Chapter 11— Places to Buy and Sale Machines....28

Chapter 12— Example Contracts 44

INTRODUCTION

In today's society, many opportunities come and go. Only the trained eye will master "The Game" and get out of what we call "The Rat Race." Businesses open and close every day, but it's a person's hunger and perseverance that prevails. The vending business is one of Americas' best-kept secrets, perhaps, raking in over a billion dollars in revenue a year. What vending can do for you will be determined by you! Vending is not a get rich scheme or an overnight success plan. There is a certain amount of energy and effort required for you to reap the benefits of becoming financially free. After reading this book, vending may or may not be an avenue you want to pursue, only trial and error will solve that issue. With that said and without further delay, let me introduce to you, America's Best Kept Secret!

CHAPTER 1
GETTING STARTED

It was a late Saturday night, and like most of us, I didn't have anything to do but watch TV. So as I glanced through the late-night programs, I happened to notice that they were airing a show that dealt with small double-head bubble gum machines. That's when the "Big Bang" idea hit me like a ton of bricks, and I knew there was a light at the end of the tunnel. My posture changed, and so did my attitude. I have always had a knack for being able to spot the diamond in the ruff. The program went on for about forty-five minutes, and I rushed to grab a pen before the number aired again. The next morning, I made the call to Cash Flow Vending to get started. They went through a series of questions about me and how I came to know about their business. I placed my first order for four double-head vending machines and found myself in business.

I patiently waited for my machines to arrive. Upon getting my machines, there was the confusion of how do I sort through all this mess. If you are like me, you are not too handy around the house when it comes to fixing things and putting them together, but one thing you can always bet on is there will be an instruction booklet for dummies lying around. After a few hours of reading and putting the machines together, the task of how do I make money in this business venture began. The public relations side of things always plays a crucial role in how well things will come together for people in the business world. If your rapport with the public isn't positive, then your business will be the same.

If anyone was more lost on how to start a business, it had to be me. I was not the best candidate for being a businessman, but I knew I could do it. The only thing that I was used to running was my apartment. Thus, I began my journey in scoping out areas in the neighborhood to place my vending machines. Most people have a complex about talking to strangers, let alone doing business with them. I used to be shy until I started forcing myself to interact with people. The most important thing about making money is location, location, location. You may have heard that adage from Ray Kroc (creator of McDonald's). You can rest assured that some parts of town are always better than others. When I began looking for places to put my vending machines, I always started out using my "gut" feeling. I was right more often than not on the placement of my machines. My motto is: "always listen to the little voice inside your head, and the God-given instincts we all have. "

I started in my neighborhood, and I found out that many people were friendly and not opposed to me placing a double-head candy machine in their establishment. The first place I went to was a beauty salon around the corner from my house. People can be uninviting when you're soliciting because they're unfamiliar with you; this is where wit and savvy sales skills come in. I have always had the gift of gab and could talk my way in or out of any situation. I approached the owner of the salon and asked if I could place a vending machine in his place of business. I told him whom I represented and the nature of my business. The man stated, "he needed a few days to think about it and that I should check back with him." I left out of the salon feeling pretty good, still knowing that there were other potential business deals to acquire, so I proceeded to another business. After a few long hours and several miles in the car, I placed three out of four machines in one day. All this may sound easy, but it wasn't. I spent lots of time and energy on getting these machines placed out into the public.

Approaching someone to place a machine may be difficult if the word "NO" scares you, in addition to initiating conversation with potential consumers. It took me some time to build up the confidence and self-esteem needed to conduct the said business. There were other business opportunities that I had been involved in that helped build that confidence. I needed to talk to someone unrestrained. The main thing that one must consider when approaching someone who is unfamiliar is a person's body language. People will let off an aura that can be felt, in turn giving you an idea of which turn to take. See, people don't like to give things away for free, so If you ask for something for free, they feel as though you should have to work for it in some form or fashion. The first five words out of your mouth should be, "How are you doing today?" Once you use the proper greeting, then the ice is broken. After that, in your most delightful voice, you should say," I work for ABC company and was wondering if we could place a candy machine in your establishment?" Give them a few seconds to respond. No matter how the answer comes out, still say, "Thank You" and move on from there. If the answer is "NO," then pick up your emotions and keep moving. If the answer is "YES," then hurry and get the candy machine in place before the person changes his or her mind! To get, you must give, and that's were percentages from the machines come in.

Most business transactions will always consist of dollars and cents for the business deal to be complete. Most owners are going to want in on the action of the profits. When people see you making money out of their business, they are going to want a piece of the pie. So, I recommend that you give them anywhere from ten to twenty percent. Always start low and increase the percentage if the person does not fall for your initial offer. The reason to leave yourself room to play is that every person is different, and you may have a person who thinks ten percent is not enough to eat on. So make sure you leave yourself a few yards to run if needed.

CHAPTER 2
WHEN THINGS GO BAD

These days it's not uncommon for someone to start out wanting to do business with you and then change their mind. Living in such an insecure world as we do, people tend to be unsure about the decisions they make on a daily basis. All could be going well, and then you get a phone call that goes something like this, "Mr. Alexander, we need you to come and remove your candy machine from our establishment. Thank you." "What in the hell just happened?" is my first thought. I received many calls like this that I felt like the bottom of my stomach was going to drop out. Naturally, I go to the place to see what all the fuss is about and come to find out it usually revolves around the money.

Most people are greedy and don't want to share in the wealth-building process. I always try to renegotiate a higher percentage because a person feels a sense of security, knowing that you want to help them make money along with you. If the increase of a percentage doesn't work, then you are left with the option to try to talk your way into a better situation. What you don't want is to have to pull the machine and lose money. There are times when none of this works, and you may have to move the machine and find a new location. When you are forced to move the machine, don't delay, get right back out there and find another spot to place your machine. You may have to store the machine in a storage space for a minute until you can run across a place to put the machine. You will experience a few down periods before you have a smooth run of things with your business.

You and the owner may not agree on things in the course of your relationship with the business owner. He or she may think a specific type of candy is better, so you may have to play along until you get your foot in the door. It's imperative that you take a survey of what people like and want to eat. Many people like to eat soft, chewy candy or chocolate, like M&Ms and Mike & Ike's. When you run into problems, do your best to make the store owner happy. Let things happen and see what transpires so that the other party knows you are willing to work with them on what they feel is best for their establishment. After the setup, if you don't see the correct amount of sales because of positioning, then make suggestions that moving the machine may help increase cash flow. You may have to move a few machines a few times to finally see a profit. Be patient, and it will happen!

CHAPTER 3
BUSINESS AFFAIRS

The essential thing in any business is the Tax I.D number. To get a Tax Identification number on your business is not a lengthy process. You need to look to your local courthouse to obtain the necessary paperwork. Depending upon what county or town you reside in, there is a fee involved in getting a license for the business.

Getting incorporated can be done in a couple of ways. You can start at your local downtown city Business Affairs office, and fill out the paperwork for a corporation, or you can go to the internet, look up the Secretary of State Business Affairs information. Once you find the correct website, look for the entity in which you would like to be registered. For example, you can register your business as a sole proprietor L.L.C (Limited Liability Corporation). A C-Corporation or S-Type Business, these are things you may have to educate yourself on when registering your business.

CHAPTER 4
ACCOUNTING

Keeping up with the books is probably one of the most tiresome and tedious parts of the job, but it's the most crucial area of your business. Record keeping is the gray area of business that allows you to see your profit, whether you are making money or not. Buying candy, buying and selling machines, or any other equipment needed for your business is part of record keeping.

You'll need several things for proper record keeping, a calculator, plenty of pencils, pens, highlighters, and a record-keeping worksheet for the location of your business' profits and losses. The accounting process can be tedious, and if you don't have the time to do your books, then you should hire someone who can. You can pay them to handle the numbers, profits, and losses of your business.

Paying taxes on your business or any business has only one process. When operating a business, you have to keep an accurate record of how you are making money versus how much you're spending. After you have your figures in place, you should be reporting this information to your Secretary of State Office monthly so your business can be accounted for without being audited. During the tax filing season, you should report all documented information to the IRS. Paying taxes may be a thorn in your backside, but it will keep you out of trouble in the long run.

CHAPTER 5
HOW DO I LOCATE PLACES FOR MY MACHINE

Locating places for vending machines can be a tedious job. You spend gas and a reasonable amount of time and energy, attempting to find places that will make some sort of profit. When it comes to locating sites for you to place your machines, the first thing to do is go to the people you know who will probably know someone who owns a business. Established relationships between people can take you further than cold calling someone you've never met and expecting them to do business with you. If you can get a good location with no stress, you are sure to make a nice profit with your small business.

In today's business, many people are forced to start from scratch. If you're like me, I didn't know where to start, nor did I have the means. You can do like many people when locating businesses, which is to drive around burning gas, energy, and walking into business after business, hoping to get the right location. That's hard work, so why not make it easy and browse the internet. The internet is an excellent resource for you to begin locating places to place your machines. Google is probably the best bet for anyone who wants fast and easy access to vending locations. In the browser, type: vending machine locations in your area and watch a wealth of information pop up. You can also type in the kind of businesses you are looking for, and that will lead to information as well. Using Google can help make life much more comfortable.

Another suggestion would be to find a vending machine locator company and have them locate companies for you. A vending locator company can be expensive, but if you have the money, it could turn out to be a profitable investment. There are several ways to find locations for your machines, but at the end of the day, it's really up to you on how you approach the market with your business.

This subject about placing machines led me to my

next issue about approaching someone to put a machine in their establishment. My philosophy is: be humble when asking people about placing a machine. Your conversation should be respectful and straightforward enough for people to understand your cause. Working from the non-profit organization side helps people feel like they are doing a good deed by allowing a non-profit company to place a machine in their establishment. If you're not aligned with a non-profit organization, you may want to consider this as an option when looking to place machines. Most businesses will allow you to place a machine in their business once they know it's for a good cause. I suggest you approach the company from this angle so you won't have any problems with getting a good location.

CHAPTER 6
LETS TALK PERCENTAGES

Talking percentages is a gray area that can sometimes raise eyebrows. The percentage given off machines usually varies from 10-20% of the total gross profit. In most cases, the owner will be fine with about fifteen percent. However, I had a situation where a principal at a school wanted sixty percent but wasn't contributing to any product. I walked away from that business deal because it wasn't in my favor.

You should never feel like you have to make less because someone wants more. Some business owners feel like they can take advantage of you if they think you're at their mercy. Never make yourself look like you need them. Always remember that you are offering a service that is comparable to none. People will have to respect you for your business skills, not your underlying desperation. In the end, percentages are what you agree upon with the business owner. You get what you negotiate-so negotiate!

CHAPTER 7
NON-PROFIT ORGANIZATION

Being a non-profit organization has many benefits in the vending business arena. In the community of business, people have and always will enjoy helping charities. You need to use this as an advantage when attempting to get clientele for your business. When walking into an establishment, you must let them know that you are working with ABC Non-Profit Organization, and you are interested in seeing about placing a vending machine in their place of business. You want to say this to the potential client because that eliminates the possible doubt they may have regarding only you profiting. Be sure to emphasize that a portion of the money goes to ABC Non-Profit Organization. You should always place a sticker on the machine of the non-profit organization you are in business with so people will know you are legitimate.

Non-profit organizations have a much higher advantage. You being a non-profit organization takes the pressure off people thinking you're a selfish, money-driven individual whose only concern is money and doesn't care about anyone else's needs. Non-profit organizations are a significant force in any business, so do yourself a favor and become a non-profit organization.

Partnering with a non-profit business can bring prosperity and wealth. If you are in the business of making money, then aligning yourself with a non-profit organization helps. You'll need to locate several non-profit organizations you think might be a good fit for you. You'll need to do your homework and check out their track record to make sure that they're reputable. After you have narrowed your selection down to three, approach these non-profit organizations with the intent of helping them in making money. Your goal should be to use their name and logo in exchange for a percentage of sales from the net sales of the machine. Many non-profit organizations will be more than happy to do business with you. Non-profit organizations are always looking for a way to make money, so making money with you should be an easy way for them to make more. If you are willing to help someone else, you are sure to be blessed, so why not help a non-profit organization!

CHAPTER 8
YOU AND THE OWNER DON'T AGREE

Business owners can cause headaches at times when it comes to the social division of how you would like things to run and how they would like something to run. In my experience as a vendor, you always want to make the business owners happy. In most cases, the business owners will usually give you a little leeway when it comes to making money with them because they want to make money too.

There are those owners who can be difficult and want to dictate every move made by you in their business. For instance, I had a drink machine in a barbershop, and things seemed to be going okay until my machine started having technical problems. Immediately, I went to work on the issue. Drinks weren't falling, and money was being lost. I had a guy come out and put a dollar bill acceptor on the machine and deal with the technical issues, but the owner was still unhappy. The machine was fixed, and things seemed to be going smoothly for a while until people started losing change again. At this point, the owner then called me irate and said, "get the machine out of my shop at once!" I told her I needed a few days to find someone to remove the machine and she started threatening me, " I will have the machine moved and put outside if you don't get this machine out of my shop!" I complied and luckily found someone that day who moved it. It cost me seventy bucks to do so.

As you can see, the owner and I had a falling out over how my vending machine was performing. You will encounter many people like this throughout your vending career, but don't let it bother you. People are people no matter who you are. Don't take things personally; just move on and look for other locations.

CHAPTER 9
STRATEGIC PLANNING

Planning is an essential component of any business. You must make the plan simple so others can see it. When starting any business, there are vital components that help the company generate profits.

Marketing, Promotions, and Sales are what's needed for any business to survive in the new millennium. My advice is to sit down and write out a plan of how you intend to attack the market. After creating your plan, you have a road map and a vision of what you need to do to win with your vending machine business.

Planning could consist of how many stores you intend to have in a set amount of days. A person looking to acquire a large number of high volume stores needs to plan what they will need to have those stores. Don't be a chicken with your head cut off. Know where you're going and stay focused. Say, for example, you want to get twenty stores a month. You'll need to write out a plan on how you will bring that into reality. It could be that you need to call a certain number of businesses a week, or you physically drive from one location to the next to meet your goal of twenty stores. Planning is the essential vitamin that's needed to help your business grow.

CHAPTER 10
CONCLUSION

Don't be alarmed; many people in this business may despise you for making money. But, your primary focus for being in this business should be to make money, provide quality service, and bring a smile to the faces of people who enjoy your products. Patience is a virtue, so take your time growing your business. In this book, I give personal testimonies of things I have done and experienced. This book will not determine how much or how little money you make; that is entirely up to you, my friend. In this business, each person will have his or her own story to tell. Don't be afraid, go out and make some money!

In closing, I hope this book gives you some basic principles to get your business off the ground and up and running. The vending business can be fun and profitable if you treat it right. Treat this business with love and care, and in return, you will reap the fruits from your labor! Many Blessings.

Thank You, Cool Water

CHAPTER 11
RESOURCES
PLACES TO BUY AND SALE MACHINES

Vending Connection
107 SE 291,hwy #220
Lee Summit, Mo 64063
800-956-8363
vendingconnection.com

Gum Balls – sale drink, snack, bubble gum. They sell candy bulk items in a wide variety.
206-284-9304 (or) 888-860-6506
www.gumballs.com
email: info@gumballs.com

Candy Machine
P.O. Box 9
San Marcos, CA 92079
Email : info@canymachines.com
760-734-1414 (or) 800-853-3941

Eagle Vending Company
100 Marble Mill court
Marietta, Ga. 30060
770-426-9969

Used Vending
60 Long Lake
Carriere, Ms 39426
Email: customerservice@usedvending.com
www.usedvending.com
601-749-8424 ext. 11

Vend Web
1735 Dameron Rd
Bessemer City, NC 28016
Email: lcreed@vendweb.com
www.vendweb.com 704-435-1466

AMS Vendors
109 West Burr Boulevard
Kearneysville, WV 25430
www.amsvendors.com
304-725-6921

East Coast Vending
678-698-7757
Email: msum367@hotmail.com

Action Incorporated Vending
Contact: Lisa Davis
Email: lisa@aactionic.com
770-922-4942

REPAIR SERVICES

Vend Net
8040 University Blvd
Des Moines, Iowa 50325
888-836-3638

The Sentinel Echo
Quality Repair Services
Knoxville, TN 37902
865-922-2876

Coin Device Service Inc.
3852 Oak Cliff Industrial Court
Atlanta, Ga. 30340
770-448-5218/ or (800) 255-9976

FIX REPAIR AND SALE AT WHOLESALE PRICES

Eagle Vending
1001 Marble Mill Court
Marietta, Ga. 30060
770-426-1926

Southern Vending
Norcross, Ga.
770-872-4412

Able Remanufacturing and Repair
Atlanta, Ga. 30303
770-922-9030

Purchase A & A Vending
A&A Global Industries
17 Stenersen Lane
Cockeysville, MD 21030
Email: bgraham@aaglobalind.com
800-638-6000

Industrial Vending
Stone Mountain, Ga.
30088 404-569-7706

CONSULTANTS

Universal Vending Consultants
19715 Oxalus court
Spring, Texas 77379
281-236-6451 (or) 877-643-8363

Pasch Consulting Group (Internet Marketing)
PMB # 12 2711 Centerville Road Ste 300
Wilmington, De 19808
Email: brain@seonj.com
732-842-4720

New Jersey Office
277 Prospect Avenue
Little Silver, NJ 07739
Email: brain@seonj.com
732-842-4720

Ari Consultants
Atlanta, Ga. 30305
404-264-1524

Master Plans
1231 New Hoyt Street, Suite 305
Portland, OR 97209
Email: Info@masterplans.com
866-557-1708

Artificially Flavored Inc.
Atlanta, Ga. 30034
Email: sevendays9@hotmail.com
678-508-4351

FINANCING

Firestone Financial 27 Christina St.
P.O.Box 610325
New, Ma 02461-0325
617-641-9274 or 800-851-1001
www.firestonefinancial.com

Liability Underwriters
1560 Indian Trail Lilburn Rd.
Norcross, Ga. 30093
Contact: Amanda McClure
Email: Amanda@liabund.com
770-242-6348

King Realty
Randall Bryan
1920 Monroe Dr. NE
Atlanta, Ga. 30324
404-942-2000

Vend Lease Company Inc.
Gary Lentz
6422 frank ford Ave
Baltimore, Maryland 21206
Email: glentz@vendlease.com
www.vendlease.net
888-363-5327

Brokers Unlimited
991 Palmetto Tyrone Rd.
Sharpsburg, Ga. 30277
Email:gregtell@brokersunlimited.com
770-463-8149 (or) 8008-699-9904

Vend More
1283 Veterans Dr.
Dalton, Ga. 30721 Contact:
Rick Sims 706-278-4653

COIN CHANGE & BILL VALIDATOR COMPANY

American Changers Corporation
1400 N.W. 65th place
Ft. Lauderdale, Fl. 33309

MeI Corporate Headquarters
1301 Wilson Dr.
West Chester, Pennsylvania
19380 610-430-2700 or 800-345-8215

Coin Co Inc.
300 Hunters Ave.
St. Louis Mo 63124
314-228-0100

Cartridge World
8075 Mall Parkway Suite 109 Lithonia, Ga. 30038
Email: lance-williams@comcast.net
www.cartridgeworldusa.com
770-484-4651

Mitchell
P.O.Box 2909
Covington , Ga. 30015
Email: Mitchell@mitchellandassoc.com
www.mitchellandassoc.com
770-788-2334 (or) 800-752-8929

JCM American Corp.
221 Rohner Ave
Akron, Oh. 44319
Email: mdennis@jcm-american.com
www.jcm-american.com
330-245-1912

COMPUTER RESEARCH CORPORATIONS FOR ROUTES

Validata
428 South Perry St.
Montgomery, Al. 36104
Email: Marketing@validata.org
www.validata.com
334-834-2324

Equipment Innovators
800 Industrial Park Dr.
Marietta, Ga.30062
Email:sales@equipmentinnovators.com
www.equipmentinnovators.com
770-427-9467 or 800-733-3434

DISTRIBUTORS

Toms
1406 old Savannah Rd.
East Dublin, Ga. 3102
478-275-8862

Kraft Foods
4000 Johns Creek Court Suite 300
Suwannee, Ga. 30024
Contact: Unita Parker
Email: Unita.parker1@kraft.com
770-459-8828

Georgia Sandwich Inc.
115 Davis Circle Suite B
Marietta, Ga. 30038
Email: mvickery@georgiasandwich.com
770-426-5678

Two Sate Vending
706-339-2042
706-863-1356
Contact: Fran Speering
Email: fran@speering.org

Quick Snack Inc.
1710 Cumberland Point Dr. #25
Marietta Ga. 30067
Contact: Moe
678-898-8831

Vistar
375 Satellite Blvd #300
Suwannee, Ga. 30024
770-447-1452 (or) 800-891-9327

GRAPHICS

Harbor Graphics
545 Timber Valley Rd.
Atlanta, Ga. 30342
Email: lee.hurdlebrink@vomela.com
www.harborgraphics.com
404-252-0877

Graphics & Screen Printing
NBS Inc.
1200 Main St.
Willston, Sc 29853
Email: bepps@nbsinc.net

BUSINESS INSURANCE

Lloyd Insurance Group
3483 Satellite Blvd
Duluth Ga. 30096
770-884-1350

Nation Wide
Liability Insurance
275 Roswell St.
Marietta, Ga. 30060
770-884-1348
www.nationwide.com

Most Choice
5600 Roswell Rd.
Atlanta, Ga. 30342
404-531-9858/ 877-601-6678
www.MostChoice.com

Liability Underwriters
1560 Indian Trail Lilburn Rd.
Norcross, Ga. 30093
Contact: Amanda McClure
Email: Amanda@liabund.com
770-242-6348

Websites
Progressive Insurance
www.progressiveinsurance.com

Liberty Mutual
www.libertymutual.com

Local Insurance
www.Localinsurance.com

Insurance Match
www.insurancematch.com

CHAPTER 12
EXAMPLE CONTRACTS

Artificially Flavored Snacks Inc. (hereafter called A.F. Snacks) was founded in 2002. The company formed on the premise of providing exceptional quality and excellent service. A.F. Snacks believes that with quality services and a great product, the customer will always be satisfied. The long-term goal for the company is to be a premier force in the community with quality products and excellent customer service. The products that we provide are top quality with guaranteed freshness in every bite.

A.F. Snacks wants to be a company of high moral ethics that serves "you" the customer and the community.

Vending America's Best Kept Secret

*This is an example of numbers based on the lowest activity

20 double headstands
Each head does $20.00/mnth
$40.00 per location

20 locations at $40.00 a site is $800.00/mnth
Non-Profits receive 10%---$960.00/yr based on 12mnths
These numbers are subject to vary according to location and public activity.

**ASK HOW YOU CAN EARN MORE!

By becoming a partner with A.F. Snacks, you are gaining access to financial abundance, risk-free with no hassles. Your non-profit organization will be able to raise money for itself without having to worry about the hassle of bookkeeping, buying products, or accounting. A.F. Snacks will handle all upfront cost of products, and placing machines in the proper locations once they are found.

Your organization will receive 10% of the total gross sales. This is an excellent opportunity for raising tax-free money for your organization without any financial or personal responsibility once the machines get placed in their proper location.

Vending America's Best Kept Secret

A.F. Snacks will be responsible for handling all paperwork and accounting for the fiscal year. After the money is collected from the machines, and an A.F. Snacks employee will count it.

Then, it will be deposited into the bank. Every quarter a check will be cut to the non-profit or for-profit corporation with accurate accounting on the collection of funds from each location.

1. Friends

2. Neighbors

3. Relatives

4. Places you work

5. Business owners you know

6. Non-profit organizations with traffic flow that you are a member of can be beneficial.

7. Churches

8. Secondary Schools- Principals, Athletic Director

***KEYNOTE---The key to this whole thing, is talking to people you have a personal relationship with, to help move the business forward. Personal relationships are worth more than their weight in gold.

The responsibility of the **non-profit organization** is to go out and locate places where these machines can get placed. Once a location is found "you" the **non-profit organization** are to have the person in charge sign off on the agreement form permitting "you" the **non-profit organization** to place a machine in their establishment. The documents are to be returned to the person in charge, making sure that names and address are on each document, who in turn gets them back to **A.F. Snacks**. Let's make this a "win-win" situation. Your non-profit logo will get displayed in the window of the machine, and you will make money with little effort.

This an agreement between the parties of (Artificially flavored) and (ABC Company) made on March 3, 2010.

1. **Professional Services**. **Artificially flavored Snacks** agrees to buy the product, do accounting, and **place vending machines in their location**.

2. **Consideration**. **Artificially Flavored Snacks** agrees to pay partner 10% of total gross sales.

3. **Designation of Duties**. The associated partner agrees to locate and place vending machines, promptly making sure that all documents are signed.

4. **Payment Terms**. Terms of payments are as follows: Payments will be made to associated partner quarterly on a calendar year giving 10% of total gross sales the associated partner has worked for in a calendar year.

Artificially Flavored Snacks

Signature: _____ **Date**: _____

Associated Partner (Organization)

Signature: _____ **Date**: _____

This is an agreement between the parties of **Artificially Flavored Snacks** and _____made on this day.

The above name, **Non-Profit Organization**, and volunteer staff responsibilities are to go out and find a location to place the vending machine promptly. Also, to have an authorized individual sign off on permission form showing names, addresses, and phone numbers of the company.

Artificially Flavored Snacks agrees to buy products, place machines in their proper location, and do accounting. The associated partner will be paid quarterly 10% of the total gross sales for a calendar year.

Artificially Flavored Snacks

Signature: _____ **Date**: _____

Associated Partner (Organization)

Signature: _____ **Date**: _____

Vending America's Best Kept Secret

This is a sample form that you can use with other businesses. Please feel free to create your own from this setup and make it happen.

Thank you

BLANK FORM

This is an agreement between the parties of _____ and _____ made on this day.

The above name **Non-Profit Organization** and volunteer staff responsibilities are to go out and find a location to place the vending machines promptly. Also, to have an authorized individual sign off on permission form showing names, addresses, and phone numbers of the company.

_____ agrees to buy products, place machines in their proper location, and do accounting. The associated partner will be paid every quarter 10% of the total gross sales for the calendar year.

Your Company:

Signature: _____ **Date**: _____

Associated Partner (Organization)

Signature: _____ **Date**: _____

This is a sample form that you can use with other businesses. Please feel free to create your own from this setup and make it happen.

Thank you

BLANK FORM

This is an agreement between the parties of _____ and _____ made on.

1. **Professional Services**. **Artificially flavored Snacks** agrees to buy the product, do accounting, and place vending machines in their location.

2. **Consideration**. **Artificially Flavored Snacks** agrees to pay partner 10% of total gross sales.

3. **Designation of Duties**. The associated partner agrees to locate and place vending machines, promptly making sure that all documents are signed.

4. **Payment Terms**. Terms of payments are as follows: Payments will be made to associated partner quarterly on a calendar year giving 10% of total gross sales the associated partner has worked for in a calendar year.

Your Company:

Signature: _____ **Date**: _____

Associated Partner (Organization)

Signature: _____ **Date**: _____

www.ingramcontent.com/pod-product-compliance
Lightning Source LLC
Chambersburg PA
CBHW050310220526
45465CB00005B/1934